A CINEMATIC HISTORY of COMEDY

www.raintreepublishers.co.uk
Visit our website to find out more information about Raintree books.

To order:
☎ Phone 44 (0) 1865 888113
🖹 Send a fax to 44 (0) 1865 314091
💻 Visit the Raintree bookshop at www.raintreepublishers.co.uk to browse our catalogue and order online.

A CINEMATIC HISTORY OF COMEDY
was produced by

David West 🧍🧍 Children's Books

7 Princeton Court
55 Felsham Road
London SW15 1AZ

Designer: Rob Shone
Editor: Rowan Lawton
Picture Research: Gail Bushnell

First published in Great Britain by
Raintree, Halley Court, Jordan Hill, Oxford OX2 8EJ, part of Harcourt Education. Raintree is a registered trademark of Harcourt Education Ltd.

08 07 06 05
10 9 8 7 6 5 4 3 2 1

ISBN 1 844 21081 2

British Library Cataloguing in Publication Data

Wilshin, Mark
 A cinematic history of comedy
 1.Comedy films - History and criticism - Juvenile literature
 I.Title
                    791.4'3617

Printed and bound in China

PHOTO CREDITS :
Abbreviations: t-top, m-middle, b-bottom, r-right, l-left, c-centre.

3, DREAMWORKS LLC / THE KOBAL COLLECTION; 4l, THE KOBAL COLLECTION; 4/5, Photo By REX FEATURES, 5r, Photo By C.UNIVERSAL/EVERETT / REX FEATURES; 6tl, Photo By SNAP / REX FEATURES; 6tr, HAL ROACH/PATHE EXCHANGE / THE KOBAL COLLECTION; 6b, Photo By EVERETT COLLECTION / REX FEATURES; 7t, THE KOBAL COLLECTION; 7m, Photo By SNAP / REX FEATURES; 7b, SNAP / REX FEATURES; 8t, Photo By SNAP / REX FEATURES; 8b, PARAMOUNT / THE KOBAL COLLECTION; 8/9t, MGM / THE KOBAL COLLECTION; 9l, Photo By EVERETT COLLECTION / REX FEATURES; 9r, Photo By EVERETT COLLECTION / REX FEATURES; 10tr, Photo By SNAP / REX FEATURES; 10b, COLUMBIA / THE KOBAL COLLECTION; 11t, COLUMBIA / THE KOBAL COLLECTION / LIPPMAN, IRVING; 11m, Photo By SNAP / REX FEATURES; 11b, Photo By SNAP / REX FEATURES; 12b, Photo By EVERETT COLLECTION / REX FEATURES; 12/13t, Photo By REX FEATURES; 13m, Photo By EVERETT COLLECTION / REX FEATURES; 13bl, UNITED ARTISTS / THE KOBAL COLLECTION; 13br, Photo By SNAP / REX FEATURES; 14m, Photo By MEL NEUHAUS/EVERETT / REX FEATURES; 14b, EALING / THE KOBAL COLLECTION; 15t, Photo By REX FEATURES; 15m, EALING / THE KOBAL COLLECTION; 15b, Photo By EVERETT COLLECTION / REX FEATURES; 18m, WARNER BROS / THE KOBAL COLLECTION; 18/19m, PARAMOUNT / THE KOBAL COLLECTION; 19t, TRI STAR / THE KOBAL COLLECTION; 19b, RANK / THE KOBAL COLLECTION; 20 t, Photo By EVERETT COLLECTION / REX FEATURES; 20b, NEW LINE / THE KOBAL COLLECTION; 21t, WARNER BROS / THE KOBAL COLLECTION; 21ml, UNITED ARTISTS / THE KOBAL COLLECTION; 21mr, Photo By SIPA PRESS / REX FEATURES; 21b, EMBASSY PICTURES / THE KOBAL COLLECTION; 22b, Photo By EVERETT COLLECTION / REX FEATURES; 22/23t, UNIVERSAL / THE KOBAL COLLECTION / VAUGHAN, STEPHEN; 22/23m, Photo By SNAP / REX FEATURES; 23m, Photo By C.20THC.FOX/EVERETT / REX FEATURES; 23b, DREAMWORKS / THE KOBAL COLLECTION; 24t, Photo By EVERETT COLLECTION / REX FEATURES; 24b, Photo By SNAP / REX FEATURES; 24/24m, PARAMOUNT/FILMWAYS / THE KOBAL COLLECTION; 25m, PARAMOUNT / THE KOBAL COLLECTION / GORDON, MELINDA SUE; 26b, THE KOBAL COLLECTION / PARAMOUNT; 26/27m, Photo By EVERETT COLLECTION / REX FEATURES; 27tr, Photo By MIRAMAX/EVERETT / REX FEATURES; 27tl, Photo By EVERETT COLLECTION / REX FEATURES; 27b, POLYGRAM / THE KOBAL COLLECTION; 28l, MONTY PYTHON FILMS / THE KOBAL COLLECTION; 28/29t, Photo By COLUMBIA/EVERETT / REX FEATURES; 29t, Photo By SONY PICS/EVERETT / REX FEATURES; 29bl, Photo By REX FEATURES; 29br, Photo By SIPA PRESS / REX FEATURES; 30l, WARNER BROS/FIRST NATIONAL / THE KOBAL COLLECTION

Every effort has been made to contact copyright holders of any material reproduced in this book. Any omissions will be rectified in subsequent printings if notice is given to the publishers.

An explanation of difficult words can be found in the glossary on page 31.

A CINEMATIC HISTORY OF COMEDY

MARK WILSHIN

CONTENTS

INTRODUCTION

*Tickling ribs and splitting sides since the birth of cinema, the comedy first hit the silver screen at the Lumière brothers' first showing of L'arroseur arrosé (1895), a comic short film, in which a young boy tricks a gardener into drenching himself with a watering hose. Soon after, comic stars such as Charlie Chaplin and Buster Keaton had audiences hooting with laughter at their slapstick gags, perfect for the **silent film** era with their physical jokes and knockabout humour. As sound arrived in cinemas, wisecrack comedies delighted audiences with their clever scripts and witty one-liners, before giving way to a flood of comic styles, ranging from screwball and spoof to gross-out gags and social **satire**. Continuing to delight cinemagoers, the comedy **genre** never grows old, always eager to coax out one more laugh.*

SILENT COMEDY GREATS

*Having honed their art on the stages of **vaudeville,** comedians like Charlie Chaplin and Buster Keaton turned to film for fame and fortune.*

COMIC GENIUS

Comedies of the silent era were centred round their star performers, like Charlie Chaplin's Little Tramp. In films such as *City Lights* (1931) Chaplin combined slapstick with genuine emotion.

THE TRAMP (1915)

Although not the first depiction of Chaplin's famous Tramp, it was in The Tramp *that Chaplin made his name as the shabby vagabond with moustache, cane and bowler hat.*

SAFETY LAST (1923)

Famous for its scene of Harold Lloyd dangling from a clock-face, Safety Last *combines daredevil stunts and comic gags, as a store clerk scales a skyscraper to impress his girlfriend.*

STEAMBOAT BILL JR (1928)

A master of physical comedy, 'The Great Stone Face' Buster Keaton plays a son trying to rescue his father 'Steamboat Bill' from jail as the city collapses beneath a cyclone.

MODERN TIMES (1936)

*Set in the industrial world of the 1930s, Modern Times sees Chaplin's Little Tramp condemned to a mental asylum and sent to jail. Chaplin uses comedy to expose the terrible conditions of the working classes during the **Great Depression.** Although filled with sound effects, singing and mechanical voices, Modern Times is considered to be the last silent film, as well as the last appearance of Chaplin's Little Tramp.*

In *The Immigrant* (1917) Chaplin focused on the struggles of the poor and in *The Great Dictator* (1940) he **satirized** Adolf Hitler. Buster Keaton used elaborate acrobatic jokes in films like *The Navigator* (1924) and *The General* (1927) to depict a hopeless dreamer trapped in a harsh world.

SILENT SLAPSTICK

The silent comic, Harold Lloyd, was more popular than Buster Keaton in his day. With a death-defying determination to succeed, Lloyd became famous for his daredevil stunts and chase sequences in movies like *The Freshman* (1925). In the **talkie** era Laurel and Hardy added comic sound effects to their slapstick routines in films such as *Way Out West* (1937).

MACK SENNETT

Known as the King of Comedy, Mack Sennett was a producer and director who discovered many stars of silent comedy, including Fatty Arbuckle and Charlie Chaplin. Made up of slapstick chases and fights, Sennett's improvised films grew less popular when sound arrived.

HOG WILD (1930)

Following Laurel and Hardy's escapades as they attempt to find Oliver's hat and fit an aerial on the roof, Hog Wild descends into chaos when their car goes careering through the city. Made at the beginning of the sound era, Hog Wild contains very little dialogue. Instead it uses visual slapstick gags to get laughs.

WISECRACK COMEDY

As sound movies hit the cinemas, the slapstick comedy of the silent era faded away. Witty wisecracks and madcap plots were popular, with musical numbers and romance routines thrown in to spice it up.

SHARP WOMEN

Like the silent greats, comic movies of the sound era were based around the talents of individual comedians. Famous for her curvy figure as well as her sharp wit, Mae West was Hollywood's most highly paid comedienne at the time. While Mae West used racy jokes and sexy dances to delight audiences in *She Done Him Wrong (1933),* the Marx Brothers had viewers in stitches with *Animal Crackers (1930)* and *Monkey Business (1931).*

A NIGHT AT THE OPERA (1935)

After the failure of their film Duck Soup *(1933), the Marx Brothers' next film introduced a plot to their wacky comedy. A* **satire** *on opera's high society,* A Night at the Opera *is famous for its crowded cabin scene.*

BELLE OF THE NINETIES (1934)

Mae West was famous for her one-liners and cheeky humour, but she suffered from censorship under the **Hays Code.** *Forced to change its title from* It Ain't No Sin, *this film outwitted the censors with its double talk, implying one thing, while meaning something else.*

I'M NO ANGEL (1933)

After the Paramount studios were saved from financial ruin with the smash hit film She Done Him Wrong *(1933), Mae West wrote* I'm No Angel, *in which she plays a mischievous circus performer. With its snappy dialogue,* I'm No Angel *shows Mae West at her funniest.*

GRUMPY MEN

Like the Marx Brothers and Mae West, W.C. Fields graduated from the **vaudeville** stage into Hollywood comedies. With a sharp tongue, W.C. Fields tickled audiences with his zany antics in *You Can't Cheat an Honest Man* (1939) and *Never Give a Sucker an Even Break* (1941). He often played grumpy husbands, taunted by children and neighbours in films such as *It's a Gift* (1934).

DUCK SOUP (1933)

In this madcap satire of war, Groucho Marx plays Rufus T. Firefly, the crazy dictator of Freedonia, who declares war on the neighbouring country of Sylvania out of love for a woman. Dismissed upon release to be a flop, Duck Soup is now considered the Marx Brothers' greatest film, with its famous mirror scene, where Harpo and Chico pretend to be Groucho's reflection.

THE BANK DICK (1940)

This film was written by the legendary comic W.C. Fields, who plays an immoral anti-hero who ends up as a detective in a bank. Fields also stars in the film as a mean drunk, who hates women, children and dogs. The Bank Dick contains sharp and cynical one-liners and a sensational car chase.

SCREWBALL

*Crackling with quick-fire **repartee**, slapstick and farcical situations, the screwball comedy is a mixture of **genres**. Depicting a war zone between men and women, the idle rich and the working classes, screwball comedies sent sparks flying with their madcap battle of wills.*

BATTLE OF THE SEXES

Beginning with *It Happened One Night* (1934) and *Twentieth Century* (1934), the screwball comedy thrived under the directors Frank Capra and Howard Hawks. Hawks focused on the battle of the sexes in *His Girl Friday* (1940) and *Bringing Up Baby* (1938) where an heiress uses her pet leopard to catch herself a husband.

IT HAPPENED ONE NIGHT (1934)

The first screwball comedy, It Happened One Night *focuses on the relationship between a wealthy socialite and a hard-nosed reporter. A feisty battle of the sexes, Capra's comedy swept the board at the first Oscar ceremony.*

FRANK CAPRA

Capra (below left) became the master of screwball comedies, pitting rich women against cunning reporters in films like Mr Deeds Goes to Town *(1936). Filmed during the **Great Depression**, Capra's comedies were inspiring and uplifting, like the Christmas favourite,* It's a Wonderful Life *(1946).*

SOME LIKE IT HOT (1959)

*Starring Jack Lemmon and Tony Curtis as two musicians who dress as women, on the run from **the Mob**. Some Like It Hot also stars Marilyn Monroe. It is still one of the most popular film comedies today.*

HIS GIRL FRIDAY (1940)

Howard Hawks' His Girl Friday sees a female reporter quit the fast life to settle down with her husband-to-be. Her scheming ex-husband, played by Cary Grant, uses every trick in the book to win her back in this screwball classic.

THE PHILADELPHIA STORY (1940)

Directed by George Cukor and starring Katherine Hepburn, The Philadelphia Story sees wealthy socialite Tracy Lord prepare for her second marriage, only for her ex-husband, played by Cary Grant, to turn up with a tabloid reporter and photographer in tow. This screwball comedy was remade as the musical High Society in 1956.

Capra, however, also explored important issues such as the Great Depression, and looked at political corruption in *Mr Smith Goes to Washington* (1939).

MODERN WOMEN

Disagreements between men and women provide the comic antics for many screwball comedies. In *The Lady Eve* (1941), a beautiful, dishonest woman on board a ship tries to seduce a rich man, and in *The Awful Truth* (1938), an almost divorced husband and wife try to ruin the other's second marriage. With women as witty and cunning as men, the screwball comedy helped promote women's rights, in films like Cukor's *The Women* (1939).

ROMANCE

Performed on the stage for centuries, the romantic comedy first hit the screens in the 1950s, following the screwball comedy. Full of misfortunes and mistaken identities, the 'romcom' focuses on people caught up in the game of love.

LOVE AND WAR

With rich party girls and womanizing men, romantic comedies of the 1950s and 1960s were a maze of masked identities. In *Roman Holiday* (1953) a runaway princess is befriended by a reporter looking for a story. In *Charade* (1963) a woman searching for her dead husband's money falls in love with a man who changes his name once a day.

AMELIE (2001)

With magical **cinematography**, Amélie follows a woman who dedicates her life to making other people happy, after she returns a box of childhood keepsakes to their owner. Marvellously mischievous, Amélie changes the lives of those around her, until she meets a man just like her.

THE SHOP AROUND THE CORNER (1940)

Ernst Lubitsch's comic masterpiece The Shop Around the Corner *follows a sales clerk in love with a woman he writes to, only to discover she's the colleague he can't stand.*

ANNIE HALL (1977)

After his break-up with actress Annie Hall, stand-up comic Alvy Singer pieces together memories of their relationship to try to work out what went wrong. Both poignant and hilarious, Woody Allen's film is based on his own real-life relationship with co-star Diane Keaton. While both actors are playing themselves, the film also explores human nature and popular culture of the 1970s. With its imaginative use of split-screens, fantasy sequences and animation to portray the emotions of the characters, Annie Hall is an award-winning masterpiece.

ROXANNE (1987)

Based on the play Cyrano de Bergerac *by Edmond Rostand, the film follows two men in love with Roxanne – one is witty and intelligent, but with a very long nose, the other handsome, but shallow and incredibly stupid.*

TOGETHER FOREVER

Modern versions of the romcom throw obstacles in the paths of the lovers, such as immigration in *Green Card* (1990), friendship in *When Harry Met Sally* (1989) and distance in *Sleepless in Seattle* (1993). In *Groundhog Day* (1993), a man living the same day over and over again slowly learns how to become his dream woman's perfect man.

BAREFOOT IN THE PARK (1967)

In Barefoot in the Park *a reserved lawyer and his free-spirited wife try to get along in their tiny Manhattan apartment.*

EALING COMEDIES

*The Ealing Studios are the oldest film studios in the world, and they gave their name to a series of comedies produced in the 1940s and 1950s. Witty and intelligent, the Ealing Comedies combined a realistic portrait of post-war London with a **satire** of British traditions and customs.*

COMEDY CAPERS

The first of the Ealing Comedies, *Hue and Cry* (1947), is a mixture of comedy and **film noir**. Filmed on location around the bomb sites of London, the film focuses on a crime lord sending out messages, by altering the wording in a comic. *Whisky Galore!* (1949) increases the laughs as the residents of a remote Scottish island plot to satisfy their whisky cravings by looting a whisky-laden ship wreck.

THE LAVENDER HILL MOB (1951)

A funny robbery film, The Lavender Hill Mob follows a timid bank clerk, planning a gold heist at his own bank. Approached by Ealing Studios, the Bank of England came up with the idea of turning the gold into miniature Eiffel towers.

PASSPORT TO PIMLICO (1949)

This film is a satire on the British government's policy of rationing supplies after World War II. It is centred round the London district of Pimlico, which declares itself independent after an un-exploded bomb unearths buried treasure.

Murder Most Foul

While many of the Ealing Comedies focused on comic crimes, *Kind Hearts and Coronets* (1949) creates comedy out of murder. When a woman is disinherited from the wealthy D'Ascoyne family, her son must murder all eight relatives who stand before him in line to the Duke's throne. The film starred the Ealing comedy regular Alec Guinness.

Alec Guinness

A stage actor before World War II, Alec Guinness made his name on the silver screen in the Ealing Comedies. With his ability to change his appearance for each role, Alec Guinness delighted audiences with the comedy Kind Hearts and Coronets, *playing all eight members of the aristocratic D'Ascoyne family.*

Kind Hearts and Coronets (1949)

The Man in the White Suit (1951)

Examining society's fear of the technological future, The Man in the White Suit *is a comic blend of satire and farce, starring Alec Guinness as the inventor of a miracle material, that won't wear out or get dirty.*

The Ladykillers (1955)

The last of the Ealing Comedies, The Ladykillers *stars Alec Guinness as Professor Marcus, who takes up lodging with the doddery old Mrs Wilberforce. Planning a robbery on a train, the gang of robbers pretend to be a band of musicians, until the little old lady uncovers the loot. Director Alexander Mackendrick's dark comedy combines a farcical plot with sinister villains, repeatedly foiled in their attempts to bump off the old lady.* The Ladykillers *was remade by the Coen Brothers in 2004.*

COMEDY OF MANNERS

*Borrowed from the theatre, the comedy of manners pokes gentle fun at the customs of a certain country or group of people. With sharp dialogue and farcical situations, this style of comedy **satirizes** all groups and cultures, from the aristocracy to modern multicultural society.*

RICH AND FAMOUS

Satirizing the lifestyle of the rich and wealthy, *Trouble in Paradise* (1932) and *La Régle du Jeu* (1939) expose the tangled relationships of the upper classes, while *Born Yesterday* (1950) focuses on a businessman who hires a journalist to make his mistress more elegant and sophisticated. Director Kusturica's unusual films *Underground* (1995) and *Black Cat, White Cat* (1998) poke fun at life in former Yugoslavia with its landscape of crime and broken dreams.

MONSOON WEDDING (2001)

A colourful portrait of a family in India, trying to cope with in-laws and weddings, Monsoon Wedding mixes Hollywood and India's Bollywood cinema to create a comedy that also examines India's struggle between tradition and modernity.

ADAM'S RIB (1949)

An unusual blend of screwball, slapstick and satire, Adam's Rib stars real-life lovers Spencer Tracy and Katherine Hepburn as lawyers on opposite sides of the courtroom. With electric dialogue between the two, both in court and at home, this 'battle of the sexes' film sparkles with comic gems.

O BROTHER, WHERE ART THOU? (2000)

Loosely based on Homer's epic poem The Odyssey, the Coen brothers' movie follows three convicts who have escaped from jail, making their way home to salvage their stashed loot. Set in the Deep South, O Brother, Where Art Thou? delights viewers with its quirky collection of oddball characters.

BRITISH COMEDY

While modern comedies set in Britain, like *Four Weddings and a Funeral* (1994) and *Love Actually* (2003), have focused on the quirky mannerisms and lovable habits of the stiff-upper-lip British, other comedies like *Bhaji on the Beach* (1993) and *East is East* (1999) have concentrated on the habits of British ethnic communities. Set in the 1970s, *East is East* depicts a family outwitting their Pakistani father, as they sidestep tradition and arranged marriages.

THE COEN BROTHERS

*Famous for their witty and dark comedies, Joel and Ethan Coen collaborate closely in the planning and making of their **black comedies**. Filled with **film noir** themes of kidnapping schemes and disastrous misunderstandings, the Coen brothers (below) combine unique visuals and witty dialogue to depict parts of the American landscape, such as the bleak North Dakota of Fargo (1996) and the Mississippi of O Brother, Where Art Thou? (2000).*

DO THE RIGHT THING (1989)

Written and directed by Spike Lee, Do the Right Thing follows the inhabitants of a multiracial Brooklyn neighbourhood on the hottest day of the year, sparked into a riot when a man notices the lack of African-Americans on the local pizzeria's wall of fame. Inspired by a real-life racist attack on black youths in a pizzeria, Do the Right Thing uses humour to examine racial tensions between different groups in a multi-ethnic community.

FORMULAS OF FUN

*Innocent dreamers and havoc-wreaking klutzes have long been comic heroes, but the innocent traveller has become a **genre** all by itself. Depicting the hilarious battle between people and their surroundings, the fish-out-of-water comedy is often used to breathe new life into traditional comedy.*

INNOCENT DREAMERS

Lost in private fantasy worlds, hopeless dreamers create hilarious chaos, with imaginary six-foot rabbits in *Harvey* (1950) and dreams of treasure-seeking adventures in *The Secret Life of Walter Mitty* (1947). Jacques Tati mastered the comedy of the unlucky fool in *Les Vacances de M. Hulot* (1953) and *Mon Oncle* (1958), where Hulot takes on the world of technology.

FAR FROM HOME

City dwellers in the wild are another form of fish-out-of-water comedies. In *Private Benjamin* (1980), a pampered high society girl survives a muddy boot camp and in *City Slickers* (1991), an executive decides to go cattle driving in the Wild West.

ROAD TO MOROCCO (1942)

Possibly the best of the Bob Hope and Bing Crosby movies, Road to Morocco is a tongue-in-cheek comedy about two pranksters loose in Morocco. Filled with slapstick humour, most of the film was improvised, including the scene of a camel spitting in Bob Hope's eye.

NATIONAL LAMPOON'S VACATION (1983)

A movie spin-off based on an article in the comic magazine <u>National Lampoon</u>, *Vacation stars Chevy Chase as a bumbling father, whose well-laid plans for a family holiday fall to pieces as the family is plagued with difficult relatives, a dead aunt, and bickering children.*

Crocodile Dundee (1986) turns the formula on its head with an Australian crocodile wrestler getting to grips with downtown New York, while the delicate comedy *Lost in Translation* (2004) depicts two Americans struggling to make sense of their lives in Tokyo, Japan.

CARRY ON CLEO (1964)

Filmed on the abandoned sets of the monumental epic Cleopatra *(1963), Carry on Cleo spoofs the Elizabeth Taylor film with a barrage of gags, puns and sexual innuendos. One of the best in the famous* Carry On *series, Carry on Cleo deals with the meeting of Julius Caesar and Cleopatra with a very British sense of humour.*

THE MUPPETS TAKE MANHATTAN (1984)

Deciding to turn their college show into a Broadway hit, the Muppets search for a producer in Manhattan. Penniless in New York, they sleep in station lockers and eat in restaurants run by rats before deciding to go their separate ways. With cameos from Hollywood stars, The Muppets Take Manhattan sees Kermit and Miss Piggy finally tie the knot.

SLAPSTICK AND FARCE

After the slapstick masterpieces of the silent era, physical comedies of the sound era combine traditional pitfalls and mishaps with the fast pace and exaggerated situations of farce. Teeming with dark secrets and mistaken identities, the modern slapstick movie soon spirals out of control.

THE BELLBOY (1960)

Written and directed by its star Jerry Lewis, The Bellboy *depicts a havoc-wreaking bellboy in a Miami hotel meeting his superstar double, Jerry Lewis.*

WREAKING HAVOC

Relying on the comic talents of the performer, slapstick comedy has made stars of clumsy buffoons. Famed for his clownish skits, Jerry Lewis reduced audiences to tears with his blundering fool in *The Bellboy* (1960), while Peter Sellers gave side-splitting performances as the incompetent detective in *A Shot in the Dark* (1964) and a clumsy actor in *The Party* (1968).

DUMB AND DUMBER (1995)

Combining the comedic talents of writer and director duo the Farrelly brothers, and its rubber-faced star Jim Carrey, Dumb and Dumber *follows two men on a road trip to Aspen, returning a suitcase of ransom money to a beautiful woman. With a string of gross gags and crazy antics, this is a modern slapstick movie.*

THE PRODUCERS (1968)

Scamming rich old ladies for money, theatre producer Max Bialystock teams up with accountant Leo Bloom to create the ultimate Broadway theatre flop and keep the ill-gotten proceeds. The two producers come up with the worst musical of all time, 'Springtime for Hitler'. Written and directed by Mel Brooks, his Oscar winning The Producers *is a riot of dark humour and bad taste.*

THE PINK PANTHER (1964)

Launching Peter Sellers as Inspector Clouseau, The Pink Panther follows the showdown between the French detective and a sophisticated jewel thief. With a jazz score by Henry Mancini, The Pink Panther is a sleek slapstick comedy.

PULLING FACES

Shooting into the spotlight with *Ace Ventura, Pet Detective* (1993), Jim Carrey stunned audiences with his rubber-faced antics. Working with the Farrelly brothers on *Dumb and Dumber* (1995) and *Me, Myself and Irene* (2000), Jim Carrey has brought a modern touch to slapstick, combining lunacy with gross-out humour, a **genre** which has come into its own with films like *There's Something about Mary* (1998).

TOOTSIE (1982)

This comedy of errors stars Dustin Hoffman as a notoriously difficult actor, who becomes the female star of a soap opera. The plot thickens when he falls in love with his female co-star.

SPOOFS

Poking fun at films from every genre, spoofs create comedy by mocking traditional movie styles. From documentaries to disaster films, the spoof knows the rules of each genre and how to get laughs flouting them.

DEAD MEN DON'T WEAR PLAID (1982)

*A tribute to **film noir**, Dead Men Don't Wear Plaid sees a private-eye investigate the murder of a cheese scientist. With footage from classic films noirs, this movie turns their dark atmosphere into light comedy.*

THIS IS SPINAL TAP (1984)

With fake interviews and mock concert footage, the spoof 'mockumentary' This is Spinal Tap documents a spandex-clad heavy metal band on their North American tour.

TONGUE IN CHEEK

Following early parodies like *Abbott and Costello Meet Frankenstein* (1948), Mel Brooks updated the genre with Yiddish-speaking Indian chiefs in his spoof *Blazing Saddles!* (1974) and crazy monsters in *Young Frankenstein* (1974).

The disaster movie came under attack in the zany comedy *Airplane!* (1980), while Brooks poked fun at *Star Wars* (1977) with his spoof *Spaceballs* (1987). Tim Burton took on 1950s sci-fi flicks with his film *Mars Attacks!* (1996), and the spy thriller was made fun of in *Austin Powers: International Man of Mystery* (1997) and *Johnny English* (2003).

THE MOCKUMENTARY

The spoof documentary, the 'mockumentary' hit the big screens with *This is Spinal Tap* (1984), establishing a trend, which carried on with obsessive dog-owners in the improvised *Best In Show* (2000) and folk musicians in *A Mighty Wind* (2003).

THE NAKED GUN (1988)

A spoof of the detective thriller, The Naked Gun *follows a feeble-minded cop floundering from one gag to another, as he attempts to save the Queen from assassination.*

TIM BURTON

Having studied animation, Tim Burton worked as a cartoonist for Disney, creating his own dark animations on the side. He was discovered and asked to direct Pee-Wee's Big Adventure *(1985). Successfully launched as a comedy director, he went on to make* Beetle Juice *(1988) and the spoof* Mars Attacks! *(1996) as well as creating imaginative black comedies, such as* Edward Scissorhands *(1990).*

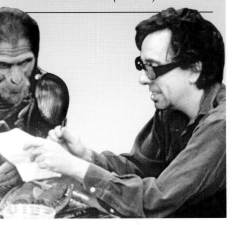

SHREK (2001) & SHREK 2 (2004)

Set in the fairytale land of Duloc, Shrek *follows the soft-hearted eight-foot ogre and his sidekick Donkey as they rescue the reluctant Princess Fiona in exchange for Shrek's swamp, now overrun with fairytale refugees.* Shrek 2 *sees the newlyweds visit Shrek's unwelcoming in-laws.* Shrek *was the first film to win the newly created animation Oscar.*

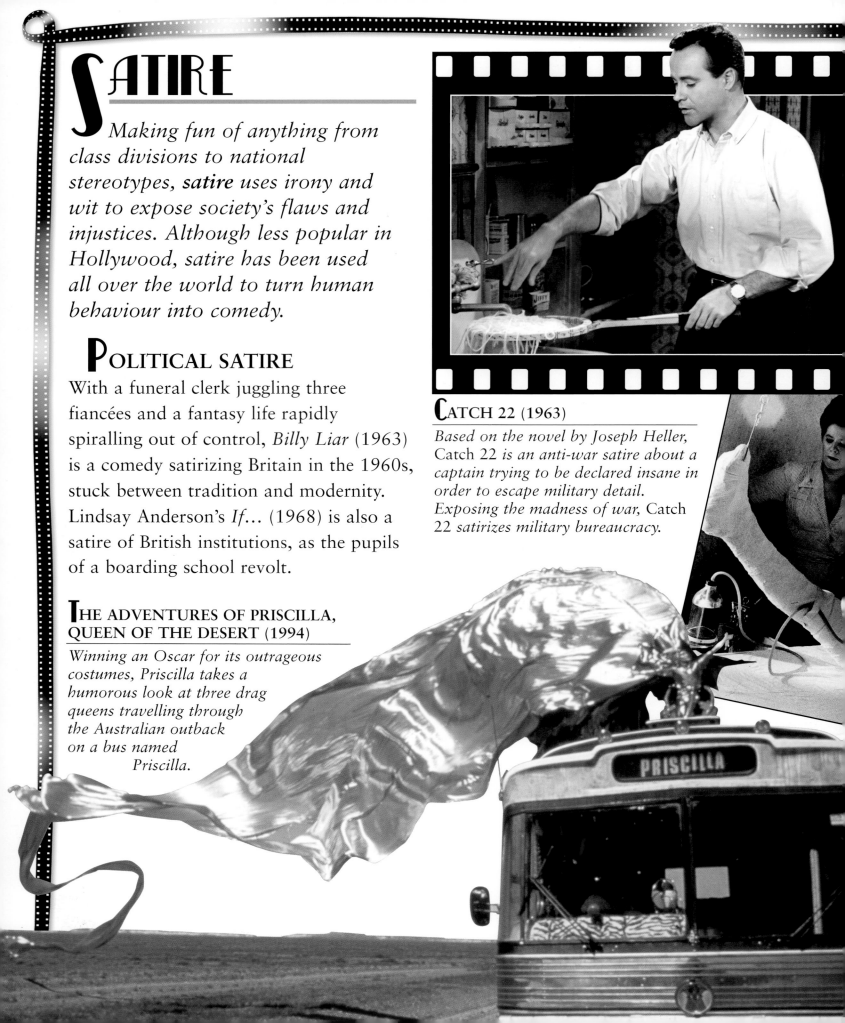

SATIRE

*Making fun of anything from class divisions to national stereotypes, **satire** uses irony and wit to expose society's flaws and injustices. Although less popular in Hollywood, satire has been used all over the world to turn human behaviour into comedy.*

POLITICAL SATIRE

With a funeral clerk juggling three fiancées and a fantasy life rapidly spiralling out of control, *Billy Liar* (1963) is a comedy satirizing Britain in the 1960s, stuck between tradition and modernity. Lindsay Anderson's *If...* (1968) is also a satire of British institutions, as the pupils of a boarding school revolt.

THE ADVENTURES OF PRISCILLA, QUEEN OF THE DESERT (1994)

Winning an Oscar for its outrageous costumes, Priscilla takes a humorous look at three drag queens travelling through the Australian outback on a bus named Priscilla.

CATCH 22 (1963)

Based on the novel by Joseph Heller, Catch 22 is an anti-war satire about a captain trying to be declared insane in order to escape military detail. Exposing the madness of war, Catch 22 satirizes military bureaucracy.

THE APARTMENT (2003)

Starring Jack Lemmon, The Apartment follows an unremarkable insurance clerk in an enormous corporation, who lends his flat to bosses and their mistresses in exchange for the chance of promotion. But when he starts to fall in love with the elevator girl, who attempts suicide in his flat after a fight with her lover, he decides to put his principles first. Directed by Billy Wilder, this dark Oscar-winning comedy satirizes the cutthroat world of business, showing how low a man will go to get ahead.

POKING FUN

While satire sometimes offers a political message, it can also be funny, like Baz Luhrmann's *Strictly Ballroom* (1992), which pokes fun at the world of ballroom dancing, or *Muriel's Wedding* (1994), a satire on small-town life in an Australian backwater. Spanish director Pedro Almodovar is famous for his social satires, with films like *What Have I Done to Deserve This?* (1984).

THE TRUMAN SHOW (1997)

A satire of reality TV, The Truman Show stars Jim Carrey as Truman Burbank, an ordinary man living a perfect life in an idyllic seaside town, who suddenly realizes his life is just a little too perfect.

ROBERT ALTMAN

Having started out in television, Robert Altman made his name with the black comedy M*A*S*H *(1970). Set in a Mobile Army Surgical Hospital during the Korean War,* M*A*S*H *satirizes the brutal effects of war. Altman's other comedies include* The Player *(1992), a satire of Hollywood filmmaking, and the Oscar-winning* Gosford Park *(2001), which satirizes the British class system of the 1930s.*

BLACK COMEDY

Using comedy to explore serious subjects like murder, drug addiction and the **atom bomb**, the black comedy tests the limits of funny movies. Breaking **taboos** and challenging stereotypes, black comedies have occasionally been banned, sometimes going beyond a joke.

LAUGHING TO DEATH

War has often been the subject of black comedies, like Lubitsch's *To Be or Not To Be* (1942), where a troupe of Polish actors try to outwit the Nazis. The **Cold War** became a comedy of errors in *Dr Strangelove or: How I Stopped Worrying and Learned to Love the Bomb* (1964), while the Oscar-winning *Life is Beautiful* (1997) brought comedy to the concentration camp, as a father tries to hide the bitter truth from his young son.

HAROLD AND MAUDE (1971)

A cult comedy classic, Harold and Maude *follows a young man obsessed with death, faking suicides and attending funerals, and a woman in her seventies with a zest for life. Dealing with taboo subjects, like suicide and war,* Harold and Maude *is an uplifting black comedy.*

DELICATESSEN (1991)

Set in a starved world, where food is so valuable it has replaced money, Delicatessen *is centred round an apartment block of cannibals, who eat dead men served up to them by the delicatessen on the ground floor. Directed by Marc Caro and Jean-Pierre Jeunet,* Delicatessen *is a bizarre black comedy.*

VIOLENTLY FUNNY

Notoriously violent, *A Clockwork Orange* (1971) is a dark comedy about a vicious troublemaker, and the government's brutal attempts to cure him. Violence is also the subject of *Buffet Froid* (1979), starring Gérard Depardieu as a man who invites his wife's murderer to dinner. Michael Lehmann's film *Heathers* (1989) is a black comedy about a young high school couple who murder most of their enemies and disguise the deaths as suicides.

THROW MOMMA FROM THE TRAIN (1987)

Starring Danny DeVito and Billy Crystal, Throw Momma from the Train is a darkly comic twist on Hitchcock's Strangers on a Train (1951). When two men decide to swap murders, a writing student kills off his professor's double-dealing wife in exchange for his nagging and bossy mother.

THE PLAYER (1992)

Starring Tim Robbins as a studio executive in charge of selecting scripts, he is blackmailed by a neglected scriptwriter until he decides to take matters into his own hands. Set in the sleazy back-stabbing world of Hollywood, Robert Altman's The Player *is both a biting satire and a black comedy about filmmaking.*

DANNY BOYLE

This British director (above right) shot to fame with his debut feature Shallow Grave *(1994), a black comedy about three friends, who turn against each other when a flatmate dies, leaving them a suitcase full of cash. Boyle followed this up with the even darker* Trainspotting *(1996), a groundbreaking comedy about a drug addict doing his best to kick the habit.*

WEIRD HUMOUR

With fantastic, **surreal** stories and a unique style, comedians with a bizarre sense of humour have created their own style of comedy. Delving into philosophical or artistic movements like **surrealism**, zany comedies create their own worlds, where normal rules do not apply.

MONTY PYTHON'S LIFE OF BRIAN (1979)

Life of Brian is a cheeky comedy about organized religion, and biblical films. Combining satire with absurd humour, this masterpiece follows Brian who is continuously mistaken for the Messiah. It also features a crazy alien invasion.

SURREAL COMEDY

'Monty Python's Flying Circus' was a TV show which aired in Britain from 1969 – 1974. The Flying Circus was made up of six men who met at university, including John Cleese, Eric Idle, Michael Palin and Terry Gilliam. The Monty Python brand of British humour has generated five films so far, all featuring the performers in a variety of roles.

BEING JOHN MALKOVICH (1999)

Directed by Spike Jonze, Being John Malkovich follows a puppeteer, who discovers a door into John Malkovich's brain, when he takes a filing job in Manhattan. Selling fifteen minutes inside Malkovich's head for two hundred dollars, Craig and his colleague Maxine make a fortune, before the real Malkovich turns up, determined to find out what's going on. Scripted by Charlie Kaufman, Being John Malkovich explores ideas of celebrity and identity, as John Malkovitch climbs inside his own mind.

LA CITÉ DES ENFANTS PERDUS (1995)

Set in a strange fantasy world of Siamese twins and killer fleas, La Cité des Enfants Perdus *follows a circus man searching for his brother and an evil scientist, who tries to steal children's dreams.*

DREAM WORLDS

Following the ultra-stylized worlds of Jeunet and Caro in *Delicatessen* (1991) and *La Cité des Enfants Perdus* (1995), other directors have dreamed up their own bizarre fantasy worlds. After *Being John Malkovich* (1999), Spike Jonze filmed *Adaptation* (2002), an off-the-wall exploration of a scriptwriter's mind, while Michel Gondry's *Eternal Sunshine of the Spotless Mind* (2004) is a quirky comedy about erased memories.

THE ADVENTURES OF BARON MUNCHHAUSEN (1988)

Overflowing with fantasy and imagination, The Adventures of Baron Munchhausen *follows an unusual aristocrat on his journey from the moon to the underworld, in a balloon made of knickers.*

LUIS BUÑUEL

After working with Salvador Dalí on his surrealist film Un Chien Andalou *(1929), Luis Buñuel directed* L'Age d'Or *(1930), a comedy satirizing religion and the middle classes. Buñuel made many satires, including* Viridiana *(1961), about a nun tormented by her uncle and the beggars she gave shelter to.*

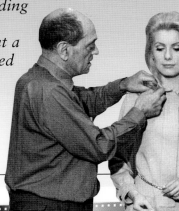

FILM TECHNOLOGY

SOUND

Warner Brothers brought sound to the screen in the 1920s with its state of the art Vitaphone process. With sound recorded on separate discs, and played alongside the film projector, Vitaphone sound was difficult to keep synchronized and was soon replaced by optical sound.

THE JAZZ SINGER (1927)

With songs and a few lines of dialogue, the first sound picture The Jazz Singer became an instant hit using the Vitaphone system.

OPTICAL SOUND

Optical sound is printed directly on the film reel. As light passes through clear soundtracks, it is turned into energy and then sound. Soundtracks can also be carried by magnetic strips like an audio cassette.

Optical analogue   Magnetic strip   Digital

SOUNDS ALL AROUND THE CINEMA

As the digital revolution picks up speed, more and more cinemas are converting to digital sound. Coded in the speckled panels between the sprocket holes, digital sound is crisp and clear. With six channels, digital sound is carried to speakers left, right and centre for dialogue, to the sub-woofer for very deep bass noises and to the surround speakers for atmospheric sounds, and to create the illusion of moving or 3D sound.

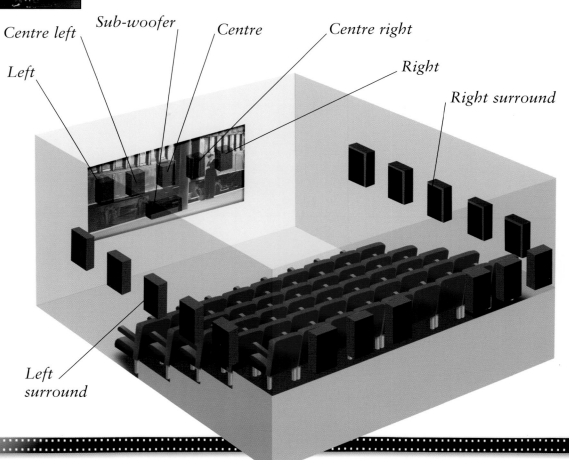

Centre left   Sub-woofer   Centre   Centre right

Left   Right

Right surround

Left surround

GLOSSARY

atom bomb
bomb whose explosive power comes from the smallest part of a chemical element that can possibly exist – an atom

cinematography
film photography and camera work

Cold War
state of hostility between nations without an actual war. The term usually describes the situation between the Soviet Union and the United States between 1945 and 1991.

film noir
film genre associated with violence and crime. Films are often set in the darkness of night with rainy streets.

genre
style or category of film, literature or art

Great Depression
economic crisis in the United States that began with the stock market crash of 1929 and continued through the 1930s

Hays Production Code
code that outlined general standards of good taste and ruled on what could and could not be shown in American films.

It was created in 1930 and enforced from 1934 onwards.

the Mob
another term used to describe the Mafia

repartee
quick, witty comments or replies in conversation

satire
when someone or something ridicules another person or thing

silent film
a film without any sound

surrealism
heightened or distorted perception of reality, by whatever means

taboo
banned or restricted by a social or religious custom

talkie
film with sound

vaudeville
entertainment featuring a mixture of comedy and musical performances

INDEX

SWEET DREAMS

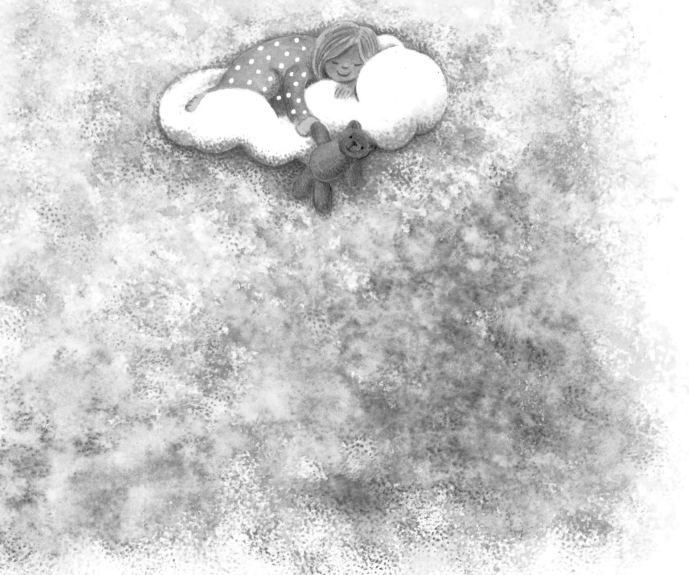

Sharing Sweet Dreams

Bedtime for little ones isn't always as peaceful as we would like! Yet it can also be a warm and loving time, when confidences are shared, the troubles and excitements of the day are resolved, and little ones fall asleep with a contentment that we can only envy.

We all know that a bedtime routine helps, and a bedtime story can be an enjoyable part of that routine for everyone. But some stories are far from soothing. *Sweet Dreams* has been specially written with peaceful bedtimes in mind.

The stories are really short, a perfect just-before-bedtime length, and most give lots of opportunities to talk with your child about his or her own experiences and share your own feelings, too.

Each story touches on a different issue—the kinds of happy and difficult emotions most children feel. You can consult the index of themes on page 80 for help in choosing an appropriate story. As each one is short, skim through it yourself first to make sure it is what you need.

Wishing you happy (and peaceful) bedtimes!   *NMAB*

SWEET DREAMS

Written by *Nicola Baxter*

Illustrated by *Pauline Siewert*

ARMADILLO

Wishing special sweet dreams to
Joshua, Poppy, Emma, Milly, Lottie, Kizzy and Shane

Published by Armadillo Books
an imprint of
Bookmart Limited
Registered Number 2372865
Trading as Bookmart Limited
Blaby Road
Wigston
Leicester
LE18 4SE

ISBN 1-84322-295-7

Produced for Bookmart Limited by Nicola Baxter
PO Box 215
Framingham Earl
Norwich Norfolk NR14 7UR

Designer: Amanda Hawkes
Production designer: Amy Barton
Editorial consultant: Sara Morling

Printed in China

Contents

The Bad Day

Once there was a little boy who had a very bad day. He didn't mean to be nasty, but somehow it just happened.

By the end of the day, everyone was grumpy. The little boy was grumpy, too. He climbed into bed and clenched his fists tight. He wanted to shout and cry.

Then someone who loved him very much sat down by the side of his bed and told him,

"When you make a mess, I love you.

When you are cross, *I love you*. When you are sad, *I love you*. When you break things, *I love you*. When you slam the door and stamp your feet, *I love you*.

I love you all day and all night.

I love you with my head and my heart and my elbows! *I love all of you*, from your funny messy hair to your funny smelly feet. And I wouldn't know what to do without you."

Then the boy lay very still, and he felt all the bad feelings slowly, slowly trickling out of his toes! And oozing out of his ears! And floating out of his fingers! And each time he breathed out, they flew out of his nose! At last, there were no bad feelings left. There was just a warm, safe feeling, like a smile inside.

"I love you, too," he said.
And the smile became a grin.
And the grin became a laugh.
And the laugh cuddled him all
night long, until it was time to
wake up to a very *good* day.

7

The Dream

Once upon a time there was a dream. It was a beautiful dream. Sometimes it was pink and orange and blue. Sometimes it was purple and red and yellow. Sometimes it was the whole rainbow—all at once!

The dream floated along, looking for someone to share its secrets. Tucked away safely inside the dream there were all kinds of wonderful things. There were stars and seashells, flowers and ice cream, rainbows and ribbons, butterflies and buses. In fact, there was everything you like best in the whole world.

Here and there the dream floated. It seemed to know which way to go. Towards the end of the day, it floated towards a window. Like magic, it flew right through the window, into the room inside.

And what did the dream find?
It found a very special person,
snuggled up in bed and
listening to a story. A story like
this one. And the dream waited,
gently bobbing up and down,
just out of sight. It waited.

When the beautiful bright eyes of the very special person
were sleepy, the dream gave a happy little sigh—and
disappeared!

*Close your eyes now, gently, gently. Wait just
a moment and you will find the dream, as
beautiful as ever, safe inside you. And before
morning comes, it will show you wonderful things.*

9

Monsters *(you know where!)*

*There were once some monsters who lived under a little girl's bed. She didn't know they were there for a long time. Then, one day, they popped into her head, and she was **sure** they were there. But she didn't dare to look.*

"I cannot go to sleep with monsters under the bed," said the little girl. "No way."

The people she loved tried to help. They peered under the bed.

"There are no monsters there at all," said one. "Go to sleep."

"Not a monster to be seen," said another. "But I have found a smelly sock."

"That is not at all the kind of place a monster likes to live," they agreed.

But the little girl could not, would not go to sleep.
"Not while there are monsters under the bed," she said,
though she was very, very sleepy and her eyes kept closing.

Then, when everyone had gone, the door slowly, slowly
opened. In came a *big* monster! The little girl was so
surprised that she wasn't even afraid.

The monster marched straight up to the bed
and peered under it. "Come out, you naughty
monsterlings!" she cried. "It's time you were
tucked up in your monster beds. Come out
this minute, and don't let me *ever*
find you there again!"

So one, two, three, little monsters
crept out and followed their monster
mother out of the room.

The little girl said to herself,
"I knew I was right." She smiled,
and she snuggled,
and she slept.

*If you have a you-know-what you-know-where,
just close your eyes, for monster mothers can
be shy. But they will solve your problem
in a second, every time.*

The Dark

T here was once a boy called Fred who was afraid of the dark.

One night Grandpa put Fred to bed.
"Good night, Fred. Sweet dreams!" he said.
He switched off the light and turned to go,
But Fred sat up. He shouted, "No!"

"Don't touch that light! It must stay on!
I don't like the dark when you are gone."
Grandpa frowned. He scratched his head.
"You'd better tell me the problem, Fred."

"In the light," replied Fred, "all my things are there.
I can see my bed, and my desk, and my chair.
But when it's dark, I can't see my bed,
And there's . . . er . . . something scary there instead."

"What kind of a something?" Grandpa frowned.
"Don't say there are horrible monsters around?"
"Monsters!" laughed Fred. "No! They're all right.
It's a scary fairy who comes every night."

"A scary fairy?" said Grandpa. "That's rare.
Where is that scary fairy, where?"
"Sometimes on my bed. Sometimes on my chair."
Fred looked worried. "She's everywhere!"

But Grandpa had met scary fairies before.
He smiled as he stood by the bedroom door.
"She's not on your chair and not on your bed,
That scary fairy is inside your head!
Send her away! She'll do what you say.
Think of a friendly fairy instead!"

Fred shut his eyes. It was dark, but not scary,
For there on his chair was a friendly fairy!
Now she looks after him every night,
And Fred is happy to turn off the light.

A Perfect Night

Once upon a time there was a perfect starry sky. Its thousands of stars glittered and shimmered. Night after night, they danced— very, very slowly—through the dark.

Under the stars, there was a moon. It shone, white and perfect, in the starry sky. Sometimes it showed a full, round face. Sometimes just a tiny sliver of silver could be seen. Each night it slid silently across the sky beneath the stars.

Below the moon, there was a planet. It was blue and green, like a perfect sparkling jewel. All night it turned, gently spinning, under the moon, beneath the stars.

On the planet, there were creatures—tiny ones and huge ones. Some of them skipped, and some of them flew. Some of them crept, and some of them swam. Sometimes they lay down and were still for a while—perfectly still—on the planet, under the moon, beneath the stars.

Among the creatures, there was a person. A little person, safe in a soft, snuggly bed. And someone who loved the little person was always near. Because that little person was perfect, too, and very, very precious. The little person slept, breathing gently, dreaming and smiling, in the warm bed, on the planet, under the moon, beneath the stars.

And all night, the stars danced, and the moon slid, and the planet turned, and the little person slept, and everything was just as it should be. Perfect.

15

The New Baby

Jake had a new baby sister. She was a happy baby. And she made everyone else happy.

Jake's parents were tired and happy.

His granny was excited and happy.

His aunties and uncles and cousins were smiley and happy. But Jake felt grim.

One night, while his dad put the baby to bed, his mother gave Jake his bath (and let him splash a little bit), and brushed his teeth (and let him squeeze the toothpaste), and snuggled him into bed. It was like old times. She said:

Once upon a time there was just me.

Then I met your dad.

I loved him with a big, big love, as high as the sky.

And I still do.

Then we knew you were coming.

As you grew inside me, the love grew, too.

We loved you with a big, big love, as high as the sky.

We still do.

When we knew that Chloe was coming, guess what happened? The love started growing again.

And it started growing in you, too.

We love her with a big, big love, as high as the sky.

And so do you.

*Then Jake was sleepy **and** happy, because he knew that it was true.*

The Wild Night

Far away, in a cave in a hillside, there lived a little bear. He was only just beginning to learn about the great, wide world.

One night, when the little bear was curled up ready to sleep, he heard a huge crash!

At the mouth of the cave, he saw a bright flash!

Then there was a whooshing, and a splashing, and it sounded as if the sky was tumbling down.

"Help!" cried the little bear.

But the big bear he lived with came and gave him a cuddle.

"Don't worry," growled the big bear.
"That's just a storm outside."

"But the crashing!" cried the little bear.

"Just thunder," said the big bear.
"But the flashing!" cried the little bear.

"Just lightning," said the big bear.

"But the splashing!" cried the little bear.

"Just rain," replied the big bear, "and the whooshing is just the wind. It's a wild night outside, all right. But do you know what is wonderful about a night like this?"

"No-o-o-o," said the little bear.

"Well, inside our warm cave, there is no crashing, no flashing, and no splashing. There isn't even any whooshing. We are safe and warm, and all that crashing and flashing and splashing and whooshing just makes us feel safer and warmer, doesn't it?"

"It does," said the little bear.
He lay down his head,
and curled up in his bed,
and fell fast asleep.

Bedtime Boogie

Stand up tall,
Wave your arms in the air.
Wiggle your bottom
And shake your hair!
Stamp your feet on the ground,
Clap your hands above your head,
Do the Bedtime Boogie
When you're ready for bed!

Stre-e-e-e-etch like a cat
From your head to your toes!
Squiggle like a snake
From your knees to your nose!
Reach to the sky
And touch the floor.
It's the Bedtime Boogie
And it's time for some more!

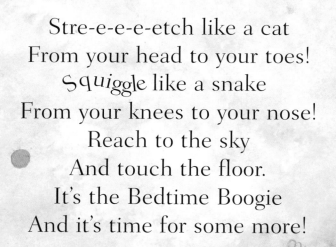

Climb into your bed
And make yourself small.
Hug yourself tight
Like a little round ball.
Then stre-e-e-e-etch out your body,
Your fingers and your toes.
You're doing the Bedtime Boogie,
And this is how it goes!

Breathe in to the rhythm
Breathe out to the beat,
Let everything go floppy
From your head to your feet.
As the Bedtime Boogie
Is almost done,
*Dance into your dreams,
My dear little one.*

Not Yet!

Each night, a little boy's dad would call, "Time to go to sleep now!" "Not yet!" the little boy would shout. "I'm busy!"

Then the boy's dad would come to the door and ask what exactly he was busy doing, and the little boy would mention just one or two things:

"I'm on a pirate ship! We're under attack. I'm worried about our parrot because his feathers are falling out. There's a mermaid under the boat who may be stealing our treasure. I've got a couple of mountains to climb, and a dragon-sighting to investigate before I can go to sleep."

There was always a lot going on in the boy's head. But even pirates with mermaid problems feel sleepy in the end. The little boy often got grumpy and tearful because he wanted badly to go to sleep but he just couldn't stop *thinking* about things.

His dad didn't know what to do with him, until one night, he happened to catch sight of an old bear at the end of the boy's bed.

"Er, does old Button do much these days?" he wondered.

"No, he just sleeps, mostly," said the boy.

"Well, I reckon too much lying around isn't good for a bear," said Dad. "Why not give him some of your trickier missions to handle? It would be good for him, and you'd be able to shut your eyes—just for a while, of course."

The boy could see that the idea had possibilities. In the nights to come, the bear climbed mountains, fought dragons, explored the ocean bed, visited the planet Saturn (twice), and rescued two children from a raging river.

And the boy had enough sleep to see him through just as many adventures . . . during the day.

23

Lullaby

(Read your child's name where there are dots. Alternate verses are for a girl or a boy to show how easy it is to change just a few words to make it work for any child. If you start with "Once there were two babies", you can read it to twins, too!)

Once there was a baby,
A wriggly, giggly baby,
And everybody loved him,
And . . . . . was his name.

Soon the baby was a toddler.
A walking, talking toddler.
And everybody loved her,
And . . . . . was her name.

Sometimes he was angry:
Pouting, *shouting* angry.
But everyone still loved him,
And . . . . . was his name.

Sometimes she was naughty:
Really *very* naughty.
But everyone still loved her,
And . . . . . was her name.

The baby is a big boy now,
A really very big boy now.
But everyone still loves him,
And . . . . . is his name.

Yes, once there was a baby,
A wriggly, giggly baby,
And everybody loves her.
We're very glad she came.

Shhhh!

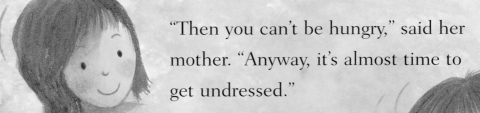

There was once a little girl who felt cross. She felt so grumpy that she couldn't talk in an ordinary voice. She **shouted!**

"I don't want to eat my dinner!"
she shouted, pushing her plate away.

"Then you can't be hungry," said her mother. "Anyway, it's almost time to get undressed."

"I don't want to get undressed!"
shouted the little girl, stamping her feet.

"Then I'll do it for you," said her mother. "Your bath is almost ready."

"I don't want to get in the bath!" shouted the little girl, hiding under a towel.

"Then I'll pick you up and put you in," said her mother. "It's almost time for bed."

"I don't want to go to bed!" shouted the little girl, sitting down.

"Then I'll have to carry you like a baby," said her mother. "It's almost time you were asleep."

"I don't want to go to sleep!" shouted the little girl with a fierce face.

"And I don't want to hear any more shouting!" shouted her mother.

"But *you're* shouting," said the little girl.

"I know!" laughed her mother. *"I'm sorry!"*

The little girl laughed. "I'm sorry, too." she said. And soon there were no more shouting sounds, just a little tiny snoring sound.

27

Staying Away

Jack's aunty took him to the park. "We'll keep out of the way until the packing's finished," she said. "Are you very excited about going to the beach?"

Jack kicked at the ground and frowned.

"What's the matter?" asked Aunty.

"What if it rains all the time?" Jack wondered.

"It *might*," Aunty laughed, "but that doesn't matter when you're in your swimming suit."

"What if the food tastes funny?" Jack was still frowning.

"Well, I suppose it *might*, but there will still be ice cream and chips and picnics," said Aunty.

Jack hadn't finished. "What if I go swimming and a shark comes and bites my toes?"

"It *might*, I suppose," said Aunty seriously. "But those toes are far too smelly for any self-respecting shark to nibble!"

"What if the hotel is really creepy and I can't get to sleep?"

"It *might* be. But everyone you love best in the world will be there with you," said Aunty. "Now, I've got a question for you.

What if you just love it?"

At last Jack smiled. "Well," he said, "I *might*."

The New House

Once there was a little girl who went into her old bedroom for the very last time.

Someone who loved her very much came in to say good night. "Tomorrow you'll be in your new room in our new house," he said. "It will be wonderful."

But the little girl sighed. "Goodbye yellow wallpaper," she said. "Goodbye stain on the carpet where I dropped my felt-tip pen and forgot to pick it up. Goodbye view from the window. Goodbye curtains that are too short since they were washed. Goodbye stars on the ceiling that Grandpa put up. Goodbye bracelet that I dropped behind the radiator and no one can get out. Goodbye best bedroom. Everything is going to be strange tomorrow night."

So then there was a little girl who went into her new bedroom for the very first time.

Someone who loved her very much came in to say good night. "How is your new room?" he said. "It looks wonderful."

And the little girl said. "Hello pink wallpaper. Hello new carpet. Hello view from the window. Hello beautiful curtains. Hello stars on the ceiling that Grandpa came specially this afternoon to put up. Hello again toys. Hello again bed."

And the person who loved her said, "You know, I like this house, but the most important thing in it is *you*, and when you put your head on your pillow—like this—and I kiss it and say good night—like this—then this isn't just a *house* any more. It's our *home*, and we're going to be happy here."

"Hello home!" said a sleepy voice. And the new house kept them safe all night long and all the nights ever after.

31

Happy Harry

Alice had a hamster called Harry. He had funny little twitchy whiskers and bright little black eyes. His silky coat was brown and white. He had tiny little toes. He was beautiful.

Alice and Harry were friends for a long time, but one day, when Alice came home from school, a grown-up she loved very much sat down with her and told her that Harry had died. "He was very old for a hamster," he said, "so he curled himself up and went to sleep. Only this time he won't wake up any more."

"You mean I'll never be able to play with him again?"

"No, not now."

"Not ever?"

"Not ever. But . . ."

"It isn't fair!" shouted Alice. "I want him back! I'll always clean out his cage if he comes back! I promise!"

"He can't come back," said the grown-up. "I know you feel grumpy and sad. But there are three very important things you must remember."

Alice looked up through her tears.

"Well, first of all, Harry had a happy life. He had his own special cage, and you took care of him so well. He was a lucky little hamster. And second of all, remember that although *you* are feeling sad and angry, Harry isn't. He is all right, and he always will be."

Alice felt a little bit better when she heard that. "And what is the third important thing to remember?" she asked.

"It's Harry!" smiled the grown-up. "We can put a picture of him on your wall, and we can talk about all the funny things he used to do. That way we will never forget him, and he can never really be gone while we still think about him."

And it was true. Harry didn't scamper on his wheel any more, but he lived in Alice's heart, and she knew that he was happy there.

33

Magic Moon

Gino's dad had to go away for a while. "You'll be fine," he told Gino. "I'll take you to Aunty May's house, and she will look after you until I get back. She really loves you."

But Gino really loved his dad. And his home. And all his toys. And his friends. He didn't want to stay with someone he could hardly remember. And deep inside, so deep he couldn't even think about it, he was worried that his dad wouldn't come back.

"I promise it will be okay," whispered Dad. "I'll be thinking about you every day."

Gino wasn't sure. The big, dark, deep worry was still there. The next day, after work, Dad put Gino's case in the car and drove him to Aunty May's house. It was a long way.

Gino looked out of the window and saw the moon, huge and white and shining. "Goodbye, Moon," he whispered.

It was very late when they arrived. Gino got out of the car, stiff and unhappy. Then he looked up. "Dad, there's a moon here as well!" he said.

"It's the same moon!" Dad laughed.

"It followed me!" Gino gasped. "All the way here!"

Dad looked down. "Yes," he said. "And you know what, it will stay with you every night until I come to get you. And the moon is even more magic than that, because it will follow me as well, to make sure I am okay, too, until I see my own boy again."

Gino suddenly felt strange and solemn and a little bit grown up. The big, dark, deep worry had gone.

So each night, he looked at the moon, and the moon looked at him. And it looked at Dad, too, far away. Until the day came when the moon looked down and smiled to see a boy and his dad —together again.

The Rainbow

It was a dark, miserable day. Allie sat by the window and watched the raindrops running down the glass. Outside, all she could see were wet rooftops and chimneys. "I hate the rain," she said. "There's nothing good about it at all."

"Well, that's not true," said her granny, who was taking care of her. "Plants need rain. Without rain, we couldn't have trees and flowers and grass to play on."

"I can't see any trees and flowers and grass up here," said Allie. She lived high up in a building in the city. "And I couldn't play on the grass today anyway. It's too wet."

"Sweetheart, don't be so miserable," said her granny. "You should try to look on the bright side. Something good always comes out of something bad. I really believe that."

Allie frowned. That was the kind of thing her granny was always saying. She didn't think it was true at all. Because of

the rain, they couldn't go out. Because of the rain, Amir
couldn't come to play. Because of the rain, she felt bored
and unhappy.

Then, around lunchtime, the rain stopped. The sun came
out. And something magical happened to the sky.

"Look at that!" cried Allie. "Look what the sun did!"

Granny grinned. "The sun couldn't do it on its own," she
said. "It needed the rain. It's like I said. Something good
always comes out of something bad."

Allie smiled, too. That was the kind of thing her granny was
always saying. Well, maybe she was right.

A Kiss Like This

Do you like kisses? Augustus did *not*!
When aunts pursed their lips,
he was off like a shot!

"I don't *want* to be smeared
With gluey lipstick!
The smell of their perfume
Makes me feel sick!

And the one with the poodle
(Who wants kisses too)
Has a face that is furry!
She should be in a zoo!

Uncle Christopher slobbers
And smells of old cheese.
Don't make me kiss him,
Or Aunt Sheila, please!"

His mother tried hard
To look stern and severe.
"Augustus, be quiet!
Now just listen here.

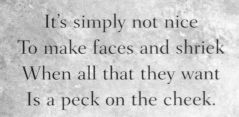

It's simply not nice
To make faces and shriek
When all that they want
Is a peck on the cheek.

But if I am truthful
I have to say this:
They are not always people
I'm eager to kiss.

You shouldn't kiss people
If it doesn't feel right,
If you shake hands instead
They will think you're polite."

That night at bedtime,
Augustus lay down
And his mother came in
With a smile *and* a frown.

"Good night, Gus," she said,
And held out her hand,
But Augustus jumped up.
"No, you don't understand!

Some kisses are awful, but yours are the best!
And a kiss like this . . . mmmm . . . is worth all the rest!"

Our Princess

One night, our mother arranged for Annie from next door to take care of us while she went to a party. We did **not** think that was right.

While our mother went to get dressed,
Annie put us in the bath.

We said:

"It isn't fair! Why can't we go to the party too?"

"Mothers don't need to go to parties. We do!"

"We don't like it when she isn't here."

"She should be taking care of *us*!"

"What if we get scared in the night?"

Annie said:

"It is a party for grown-ups."

"Your mother works hard every day.
Of course she needs to go to a party!"

"I am here to look after you.
Your mother would *never* leave you alone.
She'll come to say good night before she goes."

Annie tucked us into our beds. There was a rustle
at the door. In came someone with glittery jewels
in her ears and around her neck. And a dress that
went **woosh! swoosh!** when she walked.
And sparkly, pointy shoes. And when she leaned
over us to say good night, she smelled **wonderful!**

We said:

"*Wow!* We didn't know you
were a **princess!**
Have a great time!"

*After all, even if mothers
shouldn't go to parties,
princesses
really **should!***

41

Naughty or Not?

Robert-John did naughty things every day.
Which was the naughtiest? Can you say?

He put peanut butter in his little sister's shoes.

He scared his granny with monster shouts.

He drew on the wall (and signed his name).

He bounced on his bed—and broke it!

He walked through mud in his best shoes.

He made his mother cry.

Robert-John tried to do better.

He opened his big blue eyes wide and smiled sweetly.

He helped his little sister eat her cookies.

He got ready for bed all by himself.

He cleaned up half his bedroom.

He sat quietly while his granny brushed his hair.

He made his mother smile.

Did he succeed? What do you say?
And what was the best thing
that YOU did today?

The Good Night

There was once a princess who decided she didn't like night-time. "Take it away!" she cried. "From now on, there will only be day!"

"My dear!" The king tried to protest. He didn't think it was *possible* to take away the night.

An old woman stepped forward. She wore a purple cloak and had a round, smiling face. "I can do what the princess wishes," she said, "if she is *really* sure."

"I said so, didn't I?" the princess rudely replied.

So the old woman went outside and waited. When the shadows across the lawns were as dark and purple as her cloak, she knelt down and began to roll up the dark like a carpet. It took a long time, for the dark was everywhere.

44

When she had finished, it was daytime wherever you looked. The princess smiled. For a whole year, there was only day. Everything was always bright and busy.

Then, one day, in a high turret of the castle, the princess opened an old cupboard and found . . . a little piece of darkness left inside. It was inky blue and soft and peaceful. It felt so calm and quiet and *right* that the princess climbed inside and went to sleep.

When she woke up, she went to find the only person who could help.

"There's no need to say anything," said the old woman. "I know what you want. Perhaps you can help me."

Together, the two unrolled the night, so that it covered everything again. They stood under the stars and smiled.

"Good night, my dear," said the old woman.

"Good night," said the princess. "It really is, isn't it?"

"Oh yes," the old woman said. "The night is very good indeed."

45

The Sleepy Sea

Milly couldn't sleep. "I've got too many thoughts," she said. "My head is full of them. They won't go away."

Someone who loved Milly very much said, "Are your thoughts like butterflies, flitting lightly here and there?"

"A little bit," said Milly.

"Or are they like birds, fluttering and singing and hopping from branch to branch?"

"Not very much like birds," said Milly.

"Maybe your thoughts are like bright little fish, flashing here and there. Do they dart about, and swim and swoop, silently and smoothly in the warm, blue sea?"

"Yes," said Milly. "That's just what they're like. And they never stay still! Not even for a second!"

Then the person who loved her smiled and said, "That's because the sea is never still. Your thoughts are never still either. But when you go to sleep, you need them to be more peaceful. Shut your eyes. I'll tell you what happens."

So Milly shut her eyes and imagined a sunny sea, full of quick little fish.

She heard a quiet voice. "Look," it said. "The sun is sliding down below the sea, turning everything to gold. Now it is gone, and the water is becoming darker, deep blue under the shining moon and stars. The little fish look silver now, and as the waves roll gently across the water, the fish sway softly backwards and forwards, rocking in the warm arms of the sea. Listen, can you hear your breathing? It's like the sound of the sighing sea."

Milly drifted into sleep, and all night long, the warm sea soothed her bright little fish and kept them as still as fish or thoughts can be—until morning.

47

Christmas Eve

One Christmas, Granny came to stay. She tucked Emily into bed and read her a story. But Emily just couldn't keep still. She bounced up and said, "I'm too excited to sleep!"

Granny sighed. "Just shut your eyes and think of something wonderful."

"I **am**!" cried Emily. "I'm thinking of presents!"

"Oh, I can think of something better than that," said Granny. "And more exciting, too."

"More exciting than presents?"

"Yes," said Granny firmly. "Haven't you ever flown with the reindeer? Now shut your eyes. Imagine you are at the North Pole. It's cold there, remember. You'll need your warm blanket. Look! There's Santa's sleigh, waiting for him.

The reindeer are stamping. They want to be off. Listen!
Their bells are jingling. Quick! Climb into the back of the
sleigh and hide. Oh, here comes Santa! Keep very still!
Breathe very quietly! The sleigh is starting to move. It's
swishing across the snow! It's going faster and faster! It's
taking off! Oooooh! You're flying through the sky! The stars
are twinkling, the sleigh bells are jingling. It's the most
wonderful feeling. Keep very still. Now, where is the
sleigh going? Over forests and rivers. Over hills
and seas. Look, there are rooftops far below!"

Granny's voice was soft and warm.
She described the long, long journey.
The sleigh was heading for a
certain house. A house
Emily knew well!

Granny looked down at Emily.
She was fast asleep.
She didn't even hear
the sleigh bells jingling
just outside her window…

49

The Best Bed

Once there was a little girl who would **not** stay in her own bed. In the middle of the night her parents would hear little footsteps on the floor, and a bashing and a crashing as she flung back their door.

One day, her very sleepy dad couldn't stand it any more. "Don't you know," he said, "that every creature in the world has its own bed? I know a little elephant who has a nice bed on the ground beside a scrubby bush in Africa. And I know a parrot who sleeps on a special branch just above. I know a pony with a super stable, full of warm straw. And there's a little girl I know, not very far from here, who has a beautiful princess bed that **she should stay in!"**

"Why?" asked the little girl.

"Because," her dad replied, "if one person . . . just one person . . . starts moving about in the middle of the night, there could be terrible trouble. Suppose that pony suddenly realizes someone isn't sleeping in her beautiful princess bed? He might decide to move in himself, hoofs and all! And what if the parrot decides to sleep on the ground beside a scrubby bush? Where can that baby elephant sleep? Well, it's obvious. He will have to sleep on the special branch above. And I think that might be very bad news for the parrot!"

The little girl thought about this. She could see it made sense. So she went to sleep in her princess bed, and she stayed there all night long. (And the parrot was fine, too.)

51

Lost and Found

One night, when Giles went to bed, his mother came and sat next to him. "I want to tell you about my extraordinary day," she said. Giles was surprised. It had been a very ordinary day, he thought.

"Today," his mother began, "has been the worst day of my life. Do you remember this morning, when we went to the supermarket? You thought it would be funny to run away and hide."

"I didn't go far," said Giles.

"Oh, sweetheart, it's such a big store. I hunted everywhere for you, but I couldn't find you. I asked everyone if they had seen you. They hadn't, but they helped me to look. Then someone went to tell the manager, and he made sure that lots of people helped me."

"Everyone looking for me!" grinned Giles.
But his mother wasn't smiling.

"I was so afraid," she said.
"I kept remembering your happy
little face, and I started to cry.
I thought I might never see you
again, and I couldn't bear it."

"Don't cry now, Mama," said Giles,
because her face was looking funny.

"Then the manager himself found you near the chocolate,"
said his mother, "and he brought you over to me.
I was happy and angry all at the same time."

"I won't do it any more," said Giles.

"That's good," his mother whispered. "We'll both remember
today. The little person I love best in all the world came
back to me. So although it was the worst day I've ever
known, it was the very best day ever, too."

Staying Safe

an loved to stay with his granny. But at night, all alone in his big bed, he felt very small.

"Sweet dreams!" said Granny. "See you in the morning!"

Ian tried to smile. "What's the matter?" asked Granny.

"Dreams," said Ian in a small voice. "Sometimes."

"Ah, sometimes there are scary things?" Granny seemed to know all about it. "I knew a little girl once," she said, "who had very exciting dreams. In her dreams she climbed dragon-infested mountains and swam crocodile-infested rivers and sailed shark-infested seas. She had a wonderful time! It was great!" Granny's face had a dreamy, faraway look. "But didn't the dragons and the crocodiles and the sharks . . . you know?" asked Ian.

54

"Good gracious, no!" laughed Granny. "Of course not. She had a special shield. Not like knights of old, but a glow around her that meant dragons and crocodiles and sharks and anything else that might make dreams scary couldn't ever hurt her. She had it because lots of people loved her very much. The love protected her and kept her safe."

Ian didn't like to ask, but Granny smiled.

"Of course, you've got it too!" she cried. "Aren't you the most wonderful, most special, most loved boy in the whole wide world?"

Well, yes, Ian knew that it was true, so he set off happily into his dreams and was safe all night long.

And … just a minute! Aren't you the most wonderful, most special, most loved boy (or girl!) in the whole wide world, too? Well, that means you have the special shield, too. I bet you just can't wait to get to sleep. Sweet dreams!

Whose Bed?

Once there was a little girl who always had something to say . . . especially at bedtime! One night, her babysitter told her it was time for bed. But Lucy shouted:

"I never, ever go to bed
Without Mr. Benjamin Bingle Ted."

So Mr. Benjamin Bingle Ted
Joined little Lucy in the bed.

Then, "Wait a minute!" Lucy cried,
"I need Mrs. Bunny by my side!"

So Mrs. Bunny went in, too,
And her children—Pinky, Pumpkin and Boo.

"Wait! I'm not ready to go to sleep!
I need Humpty and Cinders and Little Bo-Peep!"

So Humpty and Cinders and Little Bo-Peep
Were squeezed into bed so that Lucy could sleep.

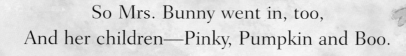

"And I need Noah and all of his crew,"
Lucy said, "and all the animals, too."

The babysitter did her best.
She tucked in Noah and all the rest.

But . . .

"Wait!" called Lucy. "Can't you see?
There isn't any room for me!"

The toys were taken out of bed
And Lucy lay down her sleepy head.

"Good night!" The babysitter hurried away . . .
Before Lucy found something else to say!

Birthday Bunny

Benny Bunny was always bouncy, but one night he was extra-super-specially bouncy. You see, he knew that next day was his birthday.

"I can't sleep!" cried Benny. "I'm too excited!" He bounced out of his bed and down the stairs.

"Back to bed, young bunny!" called his dad.

Boiiing!

Boiiing!

"I'm too excited!" shouted Benny.

"Look out!" yelled Dad.

"I feel as if I've got squiggly things in my tummy!" chortled Benny.

Boiiing!

"Benny!" Dad got bounced on! He was not a happy bunny.

"Sorry!" said Benny, but he still couldn't keep still. Nothing his mother or father said would make him go back to bed.

"Well, *we're* going to bed," said his parents at last. "If you can't go to sleep, you'll just have to stay up, Benny. See you in the morning!"

Boiing!

Benny bounced all night long. But when the sun slipped up over the windowsill in the morning, he couldn't keep his eyes open any longer. When Mr. and Mrs. Bunny came down, they found a little bunny sleeping under the kitchen table.

Benny slept . . . and slept . . . and slept. His friends came to his party, but he was still asleep. When at last he woke up, it was morning. "It's my birthday!" yelled Benny Bunny.

Dad shook his head. "That was yesterday, Benny."

Poor Benny! Of course, he opened his presents, and his friends came over for a *second* party, but it wasn't the same. When it's time for *your* birthday, make sure you go to sleep, won't you? You have to wait a whole year for the next one!

59

Sleepy Monkeys

Deep in the jungle lived two little monkeys, Chuckles and Jimble. They shared a huge tree with their parents, a snake, several parrots, two lizards and a family of frogs, but the monkeys had their own branch, of course.

The trouble started when Chuckles' and Jimble's baby sister was born. "Now boys," said their dad, "you are old enough to have your own branch. You can share that big leafy part at the end."

Chuckles and Jimble were pleased to have their own branch at last. They settled down to sleep that night feeling very grown up.

But pretty soon that branch began to bounce . . . and to wobble . . . and to jiggle. Those monkey boys had realized that out of sight of their parents they could have fun instead of going to sleep.

"Stop that right now!" called Dad.
"Don't think I can't feel that bouncing!"

The monkeys were still for a minute,
then the end of the branch started
to move suspiciously again.

"You're jiggling the whole tree!" called Dad.
"If you're not careful, you'll wake everybody up.
Chuck! Jim! Go to sleep!"

I wish I could say that those monkey boys
curled up and closed their eyes. But I can't.
They didn't listen to their father.

Next morning, Mr. Monkey swung along to the end of the
branch and found no naughty monkeys at all . . . but one
fat and sleepy snake!

Do you think the snake
had a midnight snack?
Or did he send those
monkeys to another
branch, where they
couldn't wake anyone
up? Do *you* know any
naughty monkeys who
don't go straight to sleep?

61

Get Up Now!

Once upon a time there was a lazy farmer. He knew he should get up early to start his work, but he didn't like to leave his bed. One morning, his animals gave him a surprise.

Drriiiing!

The farmer's alarm clock rang early as usual. The farmer turned it off and went back to sleep.

Clomp! Clomp! Moo!

Someone very large was coming up the stairs and into the bedroom! "It's time I was milked!" bellowed Clarice the cow.

The farmer shut his eyes tighter.

Thud! Thud! Snuffle!

Two fat, pink animals were scrambling up the stairs and across the room! "It's time for our breakfast!" snorted Polly and Wally the pigs.

The farmer snored on.

Clatter! Clatter! Baa!

Three woolly white creatures hopped up the stairs and bumped into the bed! "We need to be taken to the hillside!" bleated Daisy and Dolly and Arthur the sheep.

"Mmmnnnhmmph!" muttered the farmer.

Scritch! Scratch! Cluck!

Four angry birds fluttered up the stairs. Three landed on the farmer's head! "We want our food!" squawked Henny, Penny, Jenny and Josie the hens.

Clatter! Clatter! Baa!

The farmer sat up, still with three hens on his head, and looked around his room. He hadn't gone out to the farm, but the farm had come to him!

After that, the farmer was up bright and early every morning. Are you?

63

Noisy Toys

S ita's dad looked round the door.
"It's time to go to sleep now," he said.
"No more noise, please!"

Sita grinned. "I don't make noise!
It isn't me. It's my naughty toys!"

The clown goes bing!
The bus goes ting!
The fairy shakes her bell
With a ting-a-ling-ling!

"Come on, Sita," her dad said.
"You are the noisy one. Time for bed!"

Sita giggled. "I don't make noise!
It isn't me. It's my naughty toys!"

The drum goes bang!
The cymbal goes crash!
The cars whiz around
And go brrrm! vrrrrm! bash!

Dad looked angry and shook his head.
"You shouldn't tell fibs like that," he said.

At last sleepy Sita stopped making noise.
She climbed into bed and left her toys.

But two minutes later . . .

The clown went bing!
The bus went ting!
The fairy shook her bell
With a ting-a-ling-ling!

The drum went bang!
The cymbal went crash!
The cars whizzed around
And went brrrm! vrrrrm! bash!

Sita couldn't stop the terrible noise.
If only she hadn't blamed her toys!

Then Sita told Dad what really happened before,
And those toys were not noisy any more.

The Scary Place

Ellie didn't want to go to sleep. She didn't know why. She just didn't. But someone who loved her very much had an idea.

"It's your first day at preschool tomorrow, isn't it?" the special person asked. "Maybe you're worried that it's a scary place? It isn't, you know. Don't you remember when we went to see it? Do you know what I always do if I have to go to a scary place?"

"No," mumbled Ellie.

"Well, I go there in my head first," said the person who loved her more than the moon and stars.

Ellie frowned. "How?"

"I shut my eyes. You do it, too. That's right. Now, let's put our coats on. Hey, you've got *my* coat! This one won't fit me!"

Ellie giggled.

"OK, now here we go. We'll go in the car. Let me help with your seat belt. All right? It's not far."

Before Ellie had a chance to be scared, her special driver was saying, "We're here! Come on!" And someone with a very smiley face was saying, "Ellie! How lovely to see you! Come and put your coat here. Look, we've put your name on your peg!"

And Ellie saw some wonderful toys, and a lot of children who looked as if they really wanted to be friends. But before she was ready, someone she loved more than chocolate and ice cream said, "Time to go home now! Did you have a nice time?" And Ellie said, "Already?" But she got in the car and came home like a good girl.

Then the person who loved her said, "You know what? It's going to be just as much fun tomorrow, when you *really* go."

Ellie said, "I want to go to sleep *right now*!" And she did.

67

The Dreamboat

Sam was sad. His Dad worked on a huge ocean liner, sailing around the world all year long. When he came home, it was a very special time. Sam loved to hear stories of all the places Dad had visited. But now it was time for Dad to go again.

Sam lay in his bed and faced the wall.

"Not even going to say goodbye?" asked his dad.

Sam didn't say a word. He shut his eyes tight so that the tears wouldn't come out. But when Dad kissed him and quietly walked towards the door, he held out his arms.

"I wish you didn't have to go!
I wish I could go too!
I wish I could see all the places you see!"

Dad smiled and came back. "That's a lot of wishes, pal. I'm afraid I do have to go. You know that. But there is something you can do about the other wishes."

Sam looked up and wiped his face.

"When I was a boy," said Dad, "I longed to go to sea.
I knew it would be years and years before I could.
But every night, when I shut my eyes, I imagined all the
places I wanted to see. I called it sailing on my dreamboat."

"Did it work?" asked Sam doubtfully.

"Did it work? I went around the world six times.
And look what I do for a living now!
Of course it works! I'm ready to sail. Are you?"

"Aye, aye, Cap'n!" Sam smiled,
shutting his eyes. "I'll tell you all
about it when you get back."

"I can't wait," whispered Dad.

Magic Hugs

Once there was a little bear called Tig. He was excited when he heard he was going to stay with his cousins the Biffle boys. He knew he would have fun. But when he went to bed that first night in the Biffle house, Tig felt a funny feeling in his tummy.

"Good night, Tig," said his Aunty. "Sweet dreams!"

"Good night!" said Tig, in a small, sad voice.

Aunty put her head on one side. "Feeling homesick, Tig?" she asked. "Missing your folks at home?"

Tig nodded. He couldn't explain that bedtimes were a special time, when his big, cuddly mother and his even bigger, cuddly dad, and his three cuddly little sisters piled onto his bed and gave him a huge family hug.

Aunty sat down beside the little bear. "Do you know what I do?" she asked. "My very biggest boy has left home now. My mother and father live faraway in the mountains. My little sister, who has cubs of her own, lives overseas. But every night, before I go to sleep, I give them a magic hug."

"A magic hug?" Tig snuggled a little closer to his aunty.

"Yes, I'll tell you how to do it. You shut your eyes, and one by one you think of all the people you love who are far away. And when you've got them all together, you put a smile around them instead of your arms. A great big smile that will keep them safe until you see them again. And do you know what else I think? I'm pretty sure that at just exactly the same moment you're giving your folks a magic hug, they're giving you one right back."

So Tig shut his eyes. He thought of his mother and his dad and his sisters. Then he put a smile right around them. And as he drifted off to sleep, still smiling, he was sure he could feel big furry arms giving him a great big magic family hug, too.

Which Dream?

Close your eyes,
If you want a surprise.
Wave your finger in the air,
Let it land anywhere.
If the dream's not right, then
Try all over again!

You are a prince or princess in a beautiful castle…

You are a clown with a huge red nose…

You are a crocodile…

You are a pirate, sailing away…

You are a mermaid under the sea…

You have a pony called Midnight Star…

Everything you touch becomes a rainbow…

Your grandma has a magic wand…

When you sing, everyone starts to dance…

Your bed is a space rocket, heading for the stars……

You are a mouse…

All your toys can talk to you…

You can fly…

You're as tall as a tree…

73

All Asleep!

*F*ive little children got ready for bed,
But did they shut their eyes? No!
"We're not sleepy!" they said.

One started bouncing, hopping and jumping,
Leaping and bumping all over his bed.
His legs got wobbly, tired and wobbly,
But he wouldn't give in. "I'm not sleepy!" he said.

One started singing, chanting and humming,
Banging and strumming all over her bed.
Her voice got fainter, tired and fainter,
But she wouldn't give in. "I'm not sleepy!" she said.

One started laughing, chortling and giggling,
Wriggling and squiggling all over his bed.
His tummy got achey, tired and achey,
But he wouldn't give in. "I'm not sleepy!" he said.

One started swaying, spinning and dancing,
Twirling and prancing all over her bed.
Her arms felt heavy, tired and heavy,
But she wouldn't give in. "I'm not sleepy!" she said.

One was playing pirates, swashing and buckling,
Yo-ho-ho-ing and chuckling all over his bed.
His eyelids were drooping, tired and drooping,
But he wouldn't give in. "I'm not sleepy!" he said.

But the bouncer and singer, giggler and spinner,
And even the pirate soon crawled into bed.
They all felt sleepy, tired and sleepy,
And they had to give in. "Zzzzzzzz!" they said.

75

Sleeping Well

Once there was a little tiny girl called Poppy. She wished with all her heart that she could be bigger. One night, she told her granny that she didn't want to go to sleep.

"Why not?" Granny asked.

"I'm busy," said Poppy. She sat very still with a serious look on her face.

"Busy doing what?"

"I'm growing," said Poppy. "I need to concentrate. I haven't got time to sleep."

Granny smiled. "Oh, Poppy," she said, "you *have* to go to sleep if you are going to grow up to be a big girl!"

Poppy knew that Granny was clever as well as cuddly. She put her head on one side to listen.

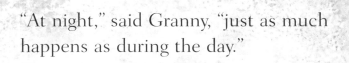

"At night," said Granny, "just as much happens as during the day."

"What happens?" asked Poppy.

"Everything!" Granny grinned.
"Your heart keeps beating.
Your body keeps breathing.
Your tummy keeps dealing with your dinner.
And most of all, you keep growing.
Your hair keeps growing.
Your nails keep growing.
All of you keeps on growing, so that every morning you are bigger and better and more beautiful than you were the day before. Though I really don't see how you *could* be more beautiful than you are today."

And Granny, that very clever, cuddly Granny, was right. Every night, the world keeps turning, and the stars keep shining, and Poppy keeps growing—and so do you!

*And tomorrow morning, you will be bigger and better and more beautiful than you are today. Though I really don't see how you **could** be more beautiful than you are today.*

Sleep well!

77

Scary Shadows

One night, Emma asked her Dad to leave the light on. Not the little light near her bed, but the big, bright light in the middle of the ceiling.

"You'll never be able to get to sleep with that on," said Dad. "What's the matter?"

"I'm scared," said Emma.

"Scared? My big beautiful girl in her pretty bed? What are you scared of?" asked Dad.

"I can't tell you." Emma opened her eyes wide to show how scared she was.

"Would it help if you whispered?" asked Dad. He knew that sometimes scary things just can't be said out loud.

Emma whispered. "There are s-s-s-scary sh-sh-sh-shadows!"

Dad looked serious. "There's only one thing to do about
that," he said. "We need to go on a scary shadow hunt.
You stay here. I'll get my equipment."

Dad came back with his big torch from the garage.
"Hold my hand," he said. "We'll do this together."

Then Dad turned off the big light.
The shadow-hunters crept around the room,
shining the torch into every corner.

"What are we doing?" whispered Emma.

"We're scaring the scary shadows," said Dad.
"Look! No shadows here, no shadows there!
Wait a minute! That *is* a scary shadow. Aaaagh!"

"That's my shadow, Dad!" Emma laughed.
"That's not scary!"

Then Dad and Emma sat on the
bed and made scary shadows and
funny shadows on the wall with
their hands, and they laughed
so much that Emma forgot to
be scared—and the shadows
forgot to be scary.

79

Choosing a Story

To dearest Bethyn
Lots of love
Grannie & Grandpa
xxx xxxx